TURNING INTO STARS

Turning into Stars

**CALIFORNIA POETS IN THE SCHOOLS
STATEWIDE ANTHOLOGY 2012**

Jackleen Holton and
Karen Lewis, Editors

Iris Jamahl Dunkle and
Dan Levinson, Field Editors

Foreword by
Juan Felipe Herrera

Copyright © 2012 California Poets in the Schools
All rights reserved. No portion of this book may be reproduced or used in any form by any means, electronic or mechanical, without prior written permission of the publisher.

Printed in the United States of America
ISBN 978-0-939927-52-4

Designer: Josef Beery
Cover art: Redwood Elementary K-2 students, led by artist Janet Self and FLOCKworks

To order copies of *Turning into Stars*, please contact:
California Poets in the Schools
1333 Balboa Street, #3
San Francisco, CA 94118
(415) 221-4201
info@cpits.org
www.cpits.org

*This book is dedicated to youth everywhere.
May your dreams, talents, and courage
create a peaceful future for all.*

Contents

Foreword: All Is the Poem *Juan Felipe Herrera*	xi
Editor's Note *Jackleen Holton*	xvii

MOTHER EARTH'S WHISPERS

Mother Earth Whispering to My Soul *Sarah Bentley*	3
A Smile of Gold *Samuel Ferguson*	5
Creek Sestina *Dane Paulson, Tessla Carlson, Sam Fanucchi, Ana Cruz, Anna Cline*	6
Metaphor Poem *Sarah Erickson*	8
Hope Is *Lillie Marie Gray*	10
My Imagination *Preeti Tamhankar*	11
Poems Hide *Kyle Tro*	12
Beautiful Place *Ezra Rubin-Clark*	13
They Call Me *Clinton Huynh*	14
I Am the Tree *Cedar Dobson*	15
Heart *Kyla Marcello*	16
Oh Nature *Ian Zalunardo*	17
Wild Fires *Wayne Delos Santos*	18
The Night's Secrets *Andrew Eliason*	19
Seasons of Gold *Julia Chen*	20
Winter *Zachary McInnis*	21
Rainbow Poetry *K'Chelle Fuller*	22
Mendocino Morning *Haley Lacey*	23

My Water Dream *Phoenix Coke*	24
Sleeping Under the Stars *Jack Scheiderman*	25
Dark Says *Cobi Napili*	26

MY OWN LITTLE HEART

The Beach with the Stars Shining Brightly *Jonah Broscow*	29
A Dazzling Heart *Lauren Stevenson*	30
Now We're Here *Ray Harris*	31
I Was Born Here / Nací Aquí *Analilia Orozco*	33
Found Poem *Mackenzie Glaubitz*	34
Small Heart *Maisie Moore*	35
Loving Dad *Victoria Castillo*	36
You *Gingko Däster*	37
Flowers *Mirian Chavez-Murillo*	39
Bright Dimension *Franklin Pierce III*	40
The Magical World *Fay Rasmuson*	42
Ode to a Pencil *Isabelle Williams*	43
My Body *Leo Johnson*	44
Who I Am . . . *Luz Hernandez*	45
I Was Born Outside *Aurora O'Greenfield*	46
What's in a Name *Lilyanna Fimrite*	47
Joy *Sam Rank*	48
Forgiveness *Heather Davis*	49
Wonderful School *Daniel Ong*	50
Eating Geometry *Raymond Ngo*	51

Mr. Rhyme and Ms. Meter *Charles Poor*	52
In Black and White *Ryan Ali*	53
The Beat of His Heart *Laurissa Simmon*	54
A Blessing *Emily Moniken*	55
Memory *Ava Nett Kruger*	56

FOREIGN FEELINGS

Learning to Drive *Sophia Zheng*	59
Confusión *Abby Gomez*	61
Rough Life *Sharon Ma*	62
Adolescence *Morgen Pack*	64
Not Mexican Enough *Raini Kellogg*	66
Hollow *Lily Chen*	67
Divorce *Lea Robbins*	69
if it makes you less sad *Cassie Spencer*	70
I Am a Fool *David*	71
Red Eyes *Ray Rhodes*	72
Black *Toni Dorin*	73
No One Knows *Monica Martell*	74
Her Eyes *Marijke Pieters-Kwiers*	75
Silence *Nyah Lund Lovergine*	77
The Caterpillar *Christopher M. Fong*	78
The Wind Is at My Back *India Allen*	79
The Starry Night *Skyla Bertsch*	80

THE WIND THAT TRAVELS THE WORLD

The Wind of the World *Parmvir Singh*	83
Slanted *Anita Chen*	84
The Moment When You Look up at the Clouds and Say "I Am" *Zoe Kaiser*	86
Joyful Dolphin / *Masaya na Lumba-Lumba* Jenna Sta. Maria	88
The Great Bird *Quinn Horak*	89
Ancestors *Ali Ali*	90
In Our Dreams *Tiffany Tang*	91
Bearded Man with a Cardboard Box *Grant Shain*	92
Red White Blue *Danin Tyrrell*	93
The Sound *Celeste Van Abrams*	94
Until I Saw *Casmali Lopez*	95
Sun of Happiness *Michael Truong*	96
The Island of a Vegetable *Rachel Chiang*	97
Polar Bear *Matthew Candau*	98
How to Be the Moon *Natasha Weiss*	99
Lighthouse Hill *Nhat Nguyen*	100
The Sun *Oceana Ortiz*	102
Chasm *Amanda Haver*	103
Raining Baseballs *Leon Wu*	104
Flyball *Cassady Komater*	105
Out of This World *Finn Baker*	106
I Am the World *Trent Johnson*	107

All Is the Poem

All is seeing. All is listening.

All is connected, yet all is always undergoing rapid transitions — from dolphin to moon, from lightning to Milky Way, from English here to ancestors there, from a singing Russian River to whale migrations and a neighboring town that wakes up when the traveling gypsy whales bask under the sea stars. All is in rapid rotation, as Analilia Orozco says:, "... *dos patrias en mi corazón* / two countries in my heart."

These poems are symphonic, celestial, deeply personal, yet this depth is sun-painted and ocean-lifted, all hope, inspiration, and sincerity — the almost-impossible goals, if we can call them that, of the poet of the twenty-first century. How can this be? These are school-age first-time writers, in most cases — with magnificent teachers, poet *maestras* and verse *maestros* — when all is writing, all is seeing, all is listening. Clear, refreshed, heart-strong, moon-strummed — real.

Back in 1981 or so, when I first jaunted into Galileo High (now the Academy of Science and Technology) in San Francisco, a few blocks from the Muni Pier, as a poet-in-the-schools poet trainee, I didn't know what I was stepping into. I peered at John Marron (my CPITS poet dojo master) in class. He took out a red plastic milk crate filled with odds and ends. A horn, a shoe, shells and strings, a clown mask, and a dog-chewed wire. "Here," he said to the students. "Pass it along." After gawking at and weighing John's found items in their hands, they wrote poems nonstop about elastic-legged surfers on a wave crest then flying from a trapeze in the sky to a ragged basketball court on the street. From that day forward, I knew CPITS was the place, the ocean, the sky, the planet where young poets would thrive and evolve. And they have.

These are stunning poems. Incredible poems. Poems that make me crazy with inner joy. I do not know if this is due to the passage of time, to the gazillion poems that I have reviewed in the last thirty years or so, or if it is due to the contrasts between what the media reports on a daily basis, you know, the violence, the bully cruelty, the forever wars, that constant rasping of human gears into broken things aching with pain and suffering. What makes this collection brilliant is not only the magnificent attention to the making, saying, and shaping of the poem, but in addition and incredibly, the heart and voice of kindness and the careful threading to family, society, human beings, and the stellar music of the galaxies. These are the new all-seeing poets that in a short time (indeed, now!) will caress and nourish our little green-brown globe. A precious California anthology.

Poems, poems, in many forms: sestinas, ekphrastic styles, found poems, short-line, long-line, poems boppin' across the page, bilingualities, odes, polylingualities, double-voiced, meditations, some with Breton and Péret's surreal palettes, others with van Gogh's thick ochre-yellow sunsets, or his starry cerulean beard unraveling across the firmament. All this is here.

I want be in these classrooms. I want to shake hands with each poet. I want to have quesadillas with all the teachers and congratulate them. And all these fresh-voiced poets across California, I want to join them; I want to dream with them as we sit in a circle of laughter and true music, the music of their lives in one magical collection.

This is a book of joy. There is room for the universe in these poems. That is why joy is possible. We go from galaxies,
> to stars,
>> to "coyotes dancing,"
>>> to "sepia-toned lovers,"
>>>> to forgiveness and friendship,
>>>>> to "a palatial mass of impossibilities,"
>>>>>> to "not Mexican enough,"
>>>>>>> to a father's "dark black and blue wings,"
>>>>>>>> to "leopards leaping,"
>>>>>>>>> to Angel Island to divorce
>>>>>>>>>> to "the flowering trees."

And the range is immense. Listen to these excerpts:

Trent Johnson, third grade — from "I Am the World":

> *I say to you, "I will never die,*
> *but this rotation is boring me."*
>
> *I dream of doing something exciting,*
> *Someday I hope to become famous.*
>
> *Be kind to me. I am the world.*

And Jenna Sta. Maria, fifth grade — from "Joyful Dolphin/*Masaya na Lumba-Lumba*":

> Ako ay isang lumba-lumba ng kasiyahan
> Natutunan kong pamunuan ang
> Mula sa paglaki ng bunan.
>
> *I am the dolphin of joy.*
> *I learned to rule the waves*
> *from the crescent moon.*

And Analilia Orozco, tenth grade — from "I Was Born Here/*Nací Aquí*":

> Todavía hay lugar
> para dos patrias en mi corazón
> > *There's still room for two*
> > *countries in my heart.*

And Anita Chen, ninth grade — from "Slanted":

> *i am the daughter of church bells echoing through the*
> > *humid air*
> *of firecrackers and sweet frozen green bean popsicles*
> *i am the daughter of slanted eyes, but they don't*
> > *undermine my vision*

Let us end with Danin Tyrrell, eleventh grade — from "Red White Blue":

> *America's lost passion*
> *Industries rise*
> *While citizens are crashing*

I thank all these brave new poets-laureate-in-the-making for writing their truth. I thank their families, teachers, schools, and their CPITS poetry *maestras* and *maestros*. I say *gracias* to John Marron for teaching me the ways of a CPITS poet. All is seeing. All is listening. All is the poem to the very last line, as Leo Johnson writes in "My Body" in his fifth-grade class: "This is the end of my poem and it is as long as I can spread my fingers."

Juan Felipe Herrera
California Poet Laureate

Editor's Note

This wondrous journey began for me the day I received the much-anticipated packet from managing editor Karen Lewis containing over three hundred of the best poems written by California students (over twenty-five thousand of them!) in CPITS poet-teacher-facilitated workshops throughout the state. But of course, it began long before that, even before my fellow poet-teachers and I stepped into our classrooms. As I contemplated the stack of poems before me, I knew that the collection was already in there somewhere, waiting to be discovered.

On my first read-through, I was concerned only with the way the light emitted from each poem. I chose my favorites quickly. A few days later, Karen and field editors Iris Jamahl Dunkle and Dan Zev Levinson weighed in with the poems that they felt needed to be included. That's when the real work began. I saw that our lenses for sensing a poem's radiance worked in vastly different ways. I revisited their favorites, holding them up to the light again.

Among the poems we loved were poems of place, both Californian and international, poems by poets of divergent cultural backgrounds, a few translations, poems of ancestry, poems of love, poems exploring nature, poems about the making of poems, and poems of sadness and grief. But the theme that kept emerging was that of a universal oneness. We all share these experiences, this world, and even what is beyond it: the seen and the unseen, the known and the unknown.

Once I discovered that the title would be *Turning into Stars*—from fourth-grader Sarah Bentley's lovely "Mother Earth Whispering to My Soul"—the collection began to assemble itself. Now, if that sounds effortless and mystical, some clarification is in order. Poems that I adored had to be turned aside, and even worse, I agonized about not being able to include poems that my fellow editors had starred as favorites. But just like that magical time of the evening when star after star blinks into sight, twinkles we had barely noticed in our first readings seemed to come from nowhere as they lit up and blazed across the sky.

I am grateful to everyone who has contributed to this anthology. Thank you to my fellow editors; to California's poet laureate Juan Felipe Herrera for his luminous foreword; to Josef Beery, our book designer; and to Carolyn Miller, our copyeditor. Thanks also go to artist-teacher Janet Self, who, along with her elementary-school students, provided the colorful cover art; to every California Poets in the Schools poet-teacher dedicated to this essential work; and to the board of directors for their vision. Gratitude to the CPITS office staff for keeping this great organization moving forward, and to every administrator and classroom teacher who welcomes poetry into his or her school. And special thanks to each donor; CPITS would not exist without their support. I am in awe of each and every young poet who takes pencil to paper and watches poetic inspiration blink on like stars from that magical place of our shared inner wisdom. We are all creative beings, coming to light.

Jackleen Holton, San Diego Poet-Teacher

MOTHER EARTH'S WHISPERS

Mother Earth Whispering to My Soul

When Mother Earth
whispers to my soul,
it is like thunder and
lightning strike my body,
but my soul takes it and
throws it out to the Milky Way.
The stars destroy it and throw a
beautiful sparkle as red as a robin.
My soul is as brave as
the first girl president.
She will run my body, and give me
good thoughts to soothe me to sleep.
But her inside is gray and lonely,
wanting someone to talk to.
It is as dark as twilight,
but the whisper from Mother Earth
isn't always bad to hear.
She has tall mountains with
strong and weak feelings, too.
She has beautiful red flowers
going up out of her into the sky
turning into stars.
Everywhere would be
dark without her.
She can throw stars
into my soul's heart
and make me bright

and happy like the
sun shining, because
everyone has
differences and comparisons.
Everyone is the same,
like Mother Earth
whispering to my soul.
She tells my soul that
everything changes,
like a hard feeling,
like a gunshot hitting glass,
falling to the ground,
making a beautiful
chiming sound.

SARAH BENTLEY
Fourth Grade, Marquez Charter Elementary School, Los Angeles County
Peggy Palo, classroom teacher
Michelle Bitting, poet-teacher

A Smile of Gold

A poem is like a shooting star
rushing through the dark blue sky.
A poem can make a gentle wind
when a fly passes by.

It is clear, fresh water
bubbling in a stream.
A poem is like an alien
shooting a laser beam.

A poem is a smile of gold
or a happy face in the clouds.
A poem likes to be quietly read,
but is happiest out loud.

SAMUEL FERGUSON
Fifth Grade, Angier Elementary, San Diego County
David Law, classroom teacher
Claudia Poquoc, poet-teacher

Creek Sestina

The creek by the big redwood,
the creek by the little bridge,
from there you always hear the sound of sticks,
the splash of frogs playing leapfrog.
The tiny creek bed is like a little canyon
with all the wildflowers pollinated by bees.

The gracious, humming bees
gather pollen from the mighty redwood.
The creek sifts through the canyon
where there is no bridge
to pass. Birds playfully join in a game of leapfrog,
while beavers build their homes with sticks.

The wonderful snap of sticks
over the beautiful buzzing sound of honeybees.
The sounds colliding or jumping over each other like leapfrog
or climbing the huge redwood
that stands in their way, but they act like it's a bridge.
They make everything seem like a canyon.

The birds soar through the canyon.
The pouring rain makes the sticks crack.
The water whirls beneath the bridge.
Small whispering, humming bees.
There is a tall redwood.
The cranes scream while playing leapfrog.

The water over rocks makes them play leapfrog
and the water echoes like a kid splashing in a canyon.
Then a huge tree growls in the canyon, a redwood.
Every step I take I hear the *crunch crunch crunch* of sticks.
I see dragonflies chasing bees,
chasing them under the bridge.

The ducks drifting under the bridge,
squirrels jumping over branches like playing leapfrog,
the smell of pollen from the bees.
Now the creek hums at the bottom of the canyon.
There are not many more sticks,
there are no more redwoods.

The never-ending redwood forest has darkened. The mystical bridge
has closed. The crunch of the sticks. Fish in the creek playing leapfrog.
The creek has drifted through the canyon. Now there is a smell of bees.

DANE PAULSON, TESSLA CARLSON, SAM FANUCCHI,
ANA CRUZ, ANNA CLINE
Fifth Grade, Prestwood Elementary School, Sonoma County
Susan Foshay, classroom teacher
Phyllis Meshulam, poet-teacher

Metaphor Poem

My hair is like
a brown wave
of whirling fog,
but my eyes
are two brown lollipops
flickering
like clouds
in the sky.
My veins are like
slithering snakes
whirling and twirling
and out of control,
but my bones are
like telephone poles
standing tall and proud.
My ears are
like two droplets
from
the dark gray clouds,
but my teeth
are butterflies
twinkling in the moon-
light.

My heart
is a symphony
of beautiful music,
but my soul
is a honeycomb
bright and sweet.

SARAH ERIKSON
Fifth Grade, Park School, Marin County
Andrea Dunn, classroom teacher
Claire Blotter, poet-teacher

Hope Is

Hope is a streaking rainbow.
Hope is clear water after a drought.
Hope is the top of a shining mountain.
Hope is a breaching dolphin.
Hope is a red balloon
swelling, rising and floating.
Hope is confidence,
wishing and knowing.
Hope is a sign of spring,
that is what hope is.

LILLIE MARIE GRAY
Third Grade, San Ramon School, Marin County
Carolyn Wainwright, classroom teacher
Terri Glass, poet-teacher

My Imagination

I am lost in the scenery of imagination,
the view of mountains,
the beautiful freshening smell of the ocean of jasmines.
I gaze at the dolphin of the moon,
how could it be so bright?

What if our world turned into a feeling?
The joy of peace enlightens me,
the courage and passion make me brave,
but the sorrow of anger scares me.

I step out of my imagination . . .
everything is gone . . .
I am left alone
all
by
my
self

PREETI TAMHANKAR
Sixth Grade, Pomeroy Elementary, Santa Clara County
Sandra Armstrong, classroom teacher
Mara Sheade, poet-teacher

Poems Hide

Poems hide in the wake
of your motorboat

Poems live on the tip
of your surfboard
doing a hang-ten as you
leap to your feet

Poems sneak under
your skimboard and wash
their hair in the water

Poems stroll into
your perfect sand castle
and feast on a sand dinner

Poems hide by the bonfire
when you're camping at the seashore

Poems ride on your back
as you bodysurf

You may not see them
or know they are there
but poems love the beach

KYLE TRO
Fourth Grade, Montecito Union School, Santa Barbara County
Heather Morales, classroom teacher
Lois Klein, poet-teacher

Beautiful Place

I walk along the beach
Toward the rocks at the other end
Huge piles of bull kelp surrounding me

I look east at the hills
Crested by redwoods
Hawks circling above

In the tidepools
I see anemones with their tendrils out
Sculpins darting through the shallow water

I hear a roar as a wave
Splashes over the mussel-covered rocks
And I think
What a beautiful place

EZRA RUBIN-CLARK
Seventh Grade, Mendocino Independent Study
Julie Brazill and Claire Skilton, classroom teachers
Emily Inwood, poet-teacher

They Call Me

They call me the mountains of water
but really I'm the tree of life,
making the undead back to life.
Some people
thank me, and others just hate me.
I'm trying to get to my friends
on the other side of the mountains.
They're so far.
Sometimes people sleep under me
while others try and cut me down.

I'm scared
they're gonna get me,
but I'll be brave.

I'm so tired, my leaves
are becoming rusty.

CLINTON HUYNH
Third Grade, Lakeshore Elementary School, San Francisco County
Patricia Arian, classroom teacher
Grace Grafton, poet-teacher

I Am the Tree

I hear the tree.
The cool wind whistles through my leaves.

I smell the tree.
My bark peels up with a sweet, sugary smell.

I see the tree.
Tall, colorful, strong and droopy.

I taste the tree.
The sweet, tangy fruit from the fruit trees.

I am the tree.
Strong, sweet, wavy, colorful, tall, proud.

CEDAR DOBSON
Fifth Grade, Oakhurst Elementary, Madera County
Sheri Clark, classroom teacher
L. Anne Molin, poet-teacher

Heart

For a year
I'm a bluebird skipping
on the treetops
For a minute
I'm a coyote dancing
in the moonlight
For a night
I'm an owl singing myself
to sleep.

KYLA MARCELLO
First Grade, Albion School, Mendocino County
Suzanne Jennings and Kathy White, classroom teachers
Karen Lewis, poet-teacher

Oh Nature

The sky is like blue streaks on paper.
The water drips.
The trees are like looming monsters.
Rushing leaves are scuttling ants trying to get to their hole.
Every creature is like a broken heart.
Swinging branches are like tigers' claws coming to get me.
Oh, the secrets of nature!
Rejoice to be hidden
forever and ever
like a pitch-black hole!

IAN ZALUNARDO
Third Grade, Gravenstein Elementary, Sonoma County
Kasey Hillier, classroom teacher
Iris Jamahl Dunkle, poet-teacher

Wild Fires

Flash!
Skies eat up hot smokes,
fire races across the plains,
devouring trees & taking lives.

My heart pounding,
it wants to escape,
but the gang of red
hangs over our exit.
Falling through a black emptiness,
I wear hot red clothes.
Black.

WAYNE DELOS SANTOS
Sixth Grade, Blackstock Junior High, Ventura County
Lisa Ayala, classroom teacher
Shelley Savren, poet-teacher

The Night's Secrets

The night is like a leaping leopard,
jumping from star to star.
It comes to meet me twice a year
but never succeeds. One day it will.
It flies like a bird, smooth as a snake
determined to meet me.
Its special power is to appear
as nothing and change back to itself.
It tells me secrets about
all the stars from the past.

ANDREW ELIASON
Third Grade, Spreckels Elementary, San Diego County
Betty Nava, classroom teacher
Celia Sigmon, poet-teacher

Seasons of Gold

Fragile leaves spin around me,
beautiful snow trails behind.
The seasons are changing rapidly,
nothing can stop them.
Aromas of pies and cakes fill the air.
Soon, the sharp smell of pine trees is mixed in.
Winter and Christmas are coming,
passing autumn and Thanksgiving.
Fall will fade, and freezing winter
will burst in like a cold wind.

These are the seasons of gold.

JULIA CHEN
Fourth Grade, La Jolla Elementary School, San Diego County
Michael Naylor, classroom teacher
Jackleen Holton, poet-teacher

Winter

I saw toboggans made of carbon
insomniac-ridden bedbugs.
The world seemed wrapped in some great white cape,
naked, virgin, beautiful, infinite.

Like tendons, rippling under ice sheets,
the water swayed to the voice of the moon.
We rode and ducked, smiling to each other
on those ice caps.
I witnessed the northern lights.

Sobbing, your tears
froze on your retina
and rivers broke to your siren's call.

ZACHARY MCINNIS
Eighth Grade, Harborside School, San Diego County
Amy Becker, classroom teacher
Jill Moses, poet-teacher

Rainbow Poetry

1.

The birds will know
I am the mountain of snow
The Russian River sang a song
whistling with the wind and whispering
I see myself as water rushing
to the shore between my eyes

2.

I am the Russian River
winding to the Pacific Ocean
I am the bright light that shines
like an eclipse of flames
I am fierce like the volcano
I am the earth of splashing colors
fading into the rainbow

K'CHELLE FULLER
Fourth Grade, Parker Elementary School, Oakland
Kathryn Mapps and Eve Scipio-Givens, classroom teachers
Maureen Hurley, poet-teacher

Mendocino Morning

The sea, the heart of the ocean beating
beating against rocks, spray shining as it flies
lifting on currents of chilled coastal air
floating toward a town
this town
nestled on the cliffs basking in the early morning light
lighting windows and rooms
The town awakes and moves
A whale spouts
Progress stops
The town sits
breath held
eyes focused
searching for that glitter of white
each crest bringing false hope
Another spout and a breach
The town exhales
The migration has started
The whales are returning

HALEY LACEY
Twelfth Grade, Mendocino Community High School, Mendocino County
Jim Jennings, classroom teacher
Emily Inwood, poet-teacher

My Water Dream

As I step into my
room I can feel
the water rising and
slowly waving
the water rises
and rises as it starts
to get colder and
colder and as the water climbs the
walls I know that I am
ready to swim and
feel the touch on my skin.

PHOENIX COKE
Third Grade, Saticoy Elementary School, Ventura County
Paula Rushing, classroom teacher
Shelley Savren, poet-teacher

Sleeping Under the Stars

Falling asleep
under the stars
I think of sea stars
gold ones
silver ones
nice ones too.
I love stars.

JACK SCHEIDERMAN
Second Grade, Lafayette Elementary School, San Francisco
Sandi Berger, classroom teacher
Susan Sibbet, poet-teacher

Dark Says

I am blackness.
I bring the moon and the stars
I give you nighttime to help you sleep
I don't need these little wings
I need to wait for my turn
The mountain of darkness is on my nose
My eyes are light but a spot of darkness
remains in my left eye
I am longer in the winter and shorter
in the summer
I hide under the table and come out at night
I am the shadows
I don't own the sun
I am most of space
I am important to earth
Together, me and light steady the temperature
To find me you have to stay up
I am the oldest thing but I am
still young

COBI NAPILI
Fourth Grade, Lakeshore Elementary School, San Francisco
Michael McCauslin, classroom teacher
Grace Grafton, poet-teacher

MY OWN LITTLE HEART

The Beach with the Stars Shining Brightly

I am the water of responsibility
I will have courage and peace
I will sizzle on the shore
I will be the king of the water
I will make only little waves
I will look up at the stars with my own little heart
The leaves of my sweet little temper
     will fall away through the hall of harmony
     and lie there until I sing to it.

I am me
and that's who I want to be.

I am the water of responsibility.

JONAH BROSCOW
Second Grade, Aurora School, Oakland
Tony Cifra, classroom teacher
Maureen Hurley, poet-teacher

A Dazzling Heart

Once I had a dream.

    I was walking through a forest
and I saw hummingbirds
singing above
        a dazzling heart.

I entered
a castle, wrapped in gold thread.
        I didn't do anything with the thread.
      I was just amazed by it.

    There was a white ribbon on the floor.
  I followed it.
It took me into a glass room
    where I heard the sound of bells.

    The dazzling heart then
called me back home
      where I saw my mom standing
          at the front door
              with her arms wide open.

LAUREN STEVENSON
Age 17, UCSF Benioff Children's Hospital, San Francisco
Kathy Evans and Sally Doyle, poet-teachers

Now We're Here
based on a family photo

Here I am,
wearing the formality my mom picked out for me.
There he is,
my new dad,
holding the hand with the new ring.
There she is,
ecstatic, holding the hand of the one she loves.
There we are,
a new family,
watching as the sun sets before us.

Here I am,
lost,
not sure what to think.
There she is,
Mom,
smiling in the limelight.
There we are,
on the Golden Gate Bridge,
dumbfounded by this occasion,
smiling.

Now we're here
at home

with a new life before us,
a new heartbeat.

There she is,
the baby,
laughing.

RAY HARRIS
Sixth Grade, Sinaloa Middle, Marin County
Patty Franklin, classroom teacher
Lea Aschkenas, poet-teacher

I Was Born Here / Nací Aquí

Nací aquí
pero mi sangre es de allá.
   I was born here
   but my blood is from there.
Soy de allá pero crecí aquí.
   I'm from there, but I grew up here.
Todavía hay lugar
para dos patrias en mi corazón.
   There's still room for two
   countries in my heart.
   I'm an assertive
   hispana,
   proud of what I am
   and anxiously awaiting
   what I will be.
Nunca olvidándome de mis raíces.
   Never forgetting my roots.
Como la rosa roja
que está en dos jardines.
   Like a rose in two gardens.
La flora aquí, pero las raíces allá.
   The flower here,
   but the roots there.

ANALILIA OROZCO
Tenth Grade, Anderson Valley High School, Mendocino County
Kim Campbell, classroom teacher
Bill Jabez Churchill, poet-teacher

Found Poem

They lower me with ropes onto rocks
Into the natural order of things
This includes the gliding eye
From the green of the earth
Which it magnifies for coolness
I'll trade a fountain pen for an outboard motor
Ask forgiveness at the end
Life's darker than circumstance
I feel happiness
I feel I'm not alone

MACKENZIE GLAUBITZ
Sixth Grade, Mill Valley Middle School, Marin County
Rod Septka, classroom teacher
Karen Benke, poet-teacher

Small Heart

My heart is a lonely
child on a swing. Deep
within my heart is love that
has never been borrowed.
My heart carries flexible
metal. My heart is made
out of old memories
that sometimes shout
out. My heart is
thirsty for
sepia-toned lovers that
once laughed but
now all that is
left is old record
players and photos.
My heart sounds
like a skipping
CD not able
to move
forward or move
back. My heart
misses what
it once had:
love to
give out, love in return.

MAISIE MOORE
Fifth Grade, Laurel Tree Charter School, Humboldt County
Brenda Sutter, classroom teacher
Dan Zev Levinson, poet-teacher

Loving Dad

I want to say your name, *Dad*.
I want you to surround me with your
dark black and blue wings.
Tell me you will never leave
my side. Fill me with
your steaming hot hugs.
I want you to recover from
your injuries so
you can be with me.
I want to say your
sweet loving name, *Dad*.
You're the one who will protect me when
I'm in danger. You
have been with me
from dusk to dawn. You
have protected me
when I'm asleep. I
want you back. *Dad*.

VICTORIA CASTILLO
Sixth Grade, Monroe Elementary School, Sonoma County
Nikki Winovich, classroom teacher
Phyllis Meshulam, poet-teacher

You

Your pale face, the freckles pale tan—
you're sick, I know—
I called, but your mother answered
and said you couldn't talk.

I wanted to tell you, remind you of the days
in your backyard picking cherries
climbing to the farthest limb
before it fell to the ground,
and behind my house adventuring,
going on long hikes on the cold, wet sand.

The time has come and gone.
Do you remember your eleventh birthday?
You tried to hit the piñata,
but you were too dizzy
and rolled down the hill.
You laughed, showing no hurt.

Do you remember paddling
in the canoe at Moonstone? I do.
We hunted for agates in the sand,
raking them with smooth sticks.

You can't see the marigolds
rising from the brown earth.
You're in bed, the white covers
over your head.

GINGKO DÄSTER
Sixth Grade, Coastal Grove Charter School, Humboldt County
Shana Langer, classroom teacher
Julie Hochfeld, poet-teacher

Flowers

We are like flowers
They blossom strong
When they battle fierce winds
Nothing can tear them down
They still stand up
Proud of what they are.

MIRIAN CHAVEZ-MURILLO
Fifth Grade, East Oakland Pride Elementary, Alameda County
Sonnie Dae, classroom teacher
Tureeda Mikell, poet-teacher

Bright Dimension

My poem isn't the darkness of clouds
It's not like a demon lurking
My poem is the bright light in your heart
I show my love and passion in my writing
I love how my poem floats smooth in the air
like a swan in the water
I believe I can fly in my imagination
and see my desires and lovely heart
I see a cloud that is gray
I pretend to fly like a bird
I love my poems and how they survive
They have the feelings of an ogre on his deathbed
My poems have tough love and a big heart
Every time I write,
I soar into my own bright dimension
I ran from my heart and lost my mind
I came back and right on time
I grew a long tail and wings and ran out to sea
I opened my passage door to a land of time,
roaring off on a bull of life
When I was born, I almost met the death angel
I ran away from the past and drifted off to the present

I see how things have changed, nothing is the same
I yell to the gods as they look down on me
I defeated hate and they gave me anger
Every day I dream of being anything I want to be
Roughness is in my heart
but I know how to control it

FRANKLIN PIERCE III
Fifth Grade, Parker Elementary School, Oakland
Alicia Martinez, classroom teacher
Maureen Hurley, poet-teacher

The Magical World

To find my house you have to walk up the big hill. You will meet a red fox. Follow him to the frog lake. The whale will come. Climb on his back. He will take you to the other side. Follow the white goose with the delicate wings. She will take you to the flowering trees. She will leave you there. Do not follow her. Instead, walk to the swirling whirlpools. When you get there, you will see a shadow. It is a red robin. Look closely. She has a cut on her head and a pink wing. Help her. When you walk a little closer you will see my house. You might find webs threaded through nature and love, and two cats in the yard. This is my house. You are welcome here forever more.

FAY RASMUSON
Third Grade, Comptche School, Mendocino County
Janna Hansen, classroom teacher
Karen Lewis, poet-teacher

Ode to a Pencil

O pencil,
you are the servant for my hand,
but the queen of all words.
Your fine point pierces the paper
and my approval,
claiming it for yourself.
Pencil, you are responsible
for my records
of past years.
It you are capable
of mistakes,
your pearly pink end
makes all evidence disappear.
You will only accept
a precise draft
and will scratch out the sloppy
and scribble in the finest
line you can create.
O jolly artist,
you are an engine
with lead as your fuel
and perfection as your motivation.
You may break,
but the words you craft
will never be destroyed,
and you will be the treasure of forever.

ISABELLE WILLIAMS
Fourth Grade, Strawberry Point School, Marin County
Anna Curtis, classroom teacher
Terri Glass, poet-teacher

My Body

I am a giant to ants in their city
My mouth is a flaming donut when I eat something spicy
My veins are highways to my heart
My bones are dead white bamboo holding me up
My head is like a bowling ball spinning on my neck
My ears blow up with golden snow the size of Paris when my
      brother annoys me
My eyes are marbles with force fields around them
My fingers are French fries roasting in the sun
My hands are smashed tennis balls from being hit really hard
My nails are like cardboard
When I wake up it's as if my hair had an explosion
The middle of my eyes are shining pennies
My muscles are a secret ghost as strong as a horse
My teeth are like claws about to smother a hamburger
My brain is a globe remembering all the states and capitals
      for the test
My lungs are an echoing balloon cave
This is the end of my poem and it is as long as I can spread
      my fingers

LEO JOHNSON
Fifth Grade, Park School, Marin County
Danny Marsh, classroom teacher
Claire Blotter, poet-teacher

Who I Am . . .

I am the one who lies to keep a smile on
        your face
The one who smiles to pretend
        everything's okay
The one who pretends everything's okay
        to keep moving on with life
The one who hides the real me
        with you because you won't
        accept who I really am
I am the one who lies to you
        and now you know
Well now you know the real me

        Take me or leave me . . .

LUZ HERNANDEZ
Ninth Grade, New Village Charter School, Los Angeles County
Cristina Medina, classroom teacher
India Radfar, poet-teacher

I Was Born Outside

I was born outside.
After three days of labor
Mom gave up the home-birth idea.
On the way to the car, I arrived.
I was raised by a pagan witch woman
and an ex-suburban, heavy-metal dude,
off the grid, on "The Land"
by sun and people.
I grew up in the land
of lizards and newts.
I was taught to look for fairies.
I discovered fingernail polish—
with sparkles!
Self-decoration is fun.
I looooove sparkles.
I created the earth in one week.
I am my own god.
I wish I could make people do
what I want them to.
My friends are like me,
at least the real ones are,
in the ways that matter.

AURORA O'GREENFIELD
Seventh Grade, Potter Valley School, Mendocino County
Jessica Hoffar, classroom teacher
Chris Olander, poet-teacher

What's in a Name

When the river starts to freeze, my name slithers out
of cracks in the ice. When the window opens into a desert,
my name blows around like a lonely scrap of paper.
It curves to the left; I run to the right. My dad calls me Tiger Lily
and picks up a yellow dandelion fluff. When I call my name,
she turns around quick and stares straight into my soul,
the grit of my life scattered around me. My name was born
in November under the moon of the falling leaves.
Sometimes she runs from me and doesn't come back.

LILYANNA FIMRITE
Fifth Grade, Tamalpais Valley School, Marin County
Robin Alderson, classroom teacher
Karen Benke, poet-teacher

Joy

Joy is being woken up in the morning
by my dog's tongue sliding across my face.
Her brown eyes as beautiful as pebbles
reflecting the morning sun.
Her tail wagging as fast as a rocket.

Joy is smelling my mom's apple muffins
fresh out of the hot oven.
It's like tasting love
made by her for me.

Joy is like winter winds blowing against my face.
Like a sparkling waterfall from a shining cloud.
I feel full of joy when I laugh
with all my heart.

SAM RANK
Third Grade, Coleman School, Marin County
Elda Parise, classroom teacher
Michele Rivers, poet-teacher

Forgiveness

Forgiveness is like a rainbow stretching across the sky,
draping the world with love.

When you forgive,
it's like millions of victory bells echoing off air.

Forgiveness is like the soft gentle wind
as it sings a faint little song of desire to forgive.

You'll never know when forgiveness will call,
blossoming from happiness.

Friendship is like forgiveness at ease,
where everybody smiles.

Forgiveness is like every graceful raindrop
that falls from the sky,
each has its own value.

HEATHER DAVIS
Third Grade, Coleman School, Marin County
Susan Artis, classroom teacher
Michele Rivers, poet-teacher

Wonderful School

School is like a hiccup of education.
It polliwogs your mind with hatches of thoughts.
School gives you a question mark right
in your head.
It gives you a scroll of thoughts waiting
to be snuggled in your breath.
It gives you an invisible sleuth to find information.

DANIEL ONG
Fifth Grade, Hoover Elementary School, Santa Clara County
Heather Buddie, classroom teacher
Gail Newman, poet-teacher

Eating Geometry

When I cut the dough,
I saw that I could make
a square, a triangle, a star.

When I finished,
I looked at the pizza,
imagining other possible shapes.

The spicy pepperoni, a very tasty circle.
The stinky onion, a very smelly square.

Then I looked at the crust, cut a triangle
out of its circle and crunched into it.
Yum! That tasted great!

What a great shape I just ate.
Hope you don't mind if I have a second piece
so I can eat another tasty geometry lesson.

RAYMOND NGO
Fifth Grade, Angier Elementary, San Diego County
Jessica Meier, classroom teacher
Claudia Poquoc, poet-teacher

Mr. Rhyme and Ms. Meter

Mr. Rhyme was going to work one day
when he met Ms. Meter. They talked
until they realized they were late for work
so they hurried up to Corporation, Inc.
They hadn't realized that Ms. Meter
was the cubicle farmer right next to him.
He invited Ms. Meter over for dinner.
Two months later they got married.
Two years later they had a baby.
They named him what they had to—Poetry!

CHARLES POOR
Third Grade, Spreckels Elementary, San Diego County
Michelle Lovern, classroom teacher
Celia Sigmon, poet-teacher

In Black and White

It starts with a mismatched pair
of socks—one red, one white.
And deepens into a silver trail
of frosty twilight.
It quickly turns into a snapshot
of the sweat and tears of a miracle.
As I open the pathway to the life
I never dreamed of, swirls surround me.
The only thing to say is a heartbreaking
story to untie the knot inside me,
unleashing waves of calm polka dots
and apples in a tree—like the echoes
of the life and journey of a poem.

RYAN ALI
Fifth Grade, Tamalpais Valley School, Marin County
Keri Wolthausen, classroom teacher
Karen Benke, poet-teacher

The Beat of His Heart

The beat of his heart is music to my ears.
The downbeat of his heart will sing me to sleep.
The tone of his melody is sweet and soothing.
His chord begins the orchestra
and when the vibration begins to rock,
his tempo minors and sharps.
As the meter begins to fret,
phrases become flat
and his musical song begins to slow,
the rhythm of the beat disappears.
Slowly, I sing my own orchestra of sleep.

LAURISSA SIMMONS
Eleventh Grade, South Valley High School, Mendocino County
David Bigelman, classroom teacher
Chris Olander, poet-teacher

A Blessing

Hungry baby loudly calling to its mother
    make it last

colorful wildflowers blooming
    make them last

the sweet taste of red raspberries
    make it last

dragonflies glistening in the bright yellow sun
    make it last

sightings of big water beetles on the secret pond
    make them last

us playing together
    make it last

EMILY MONIKEN
Age 12, UCSF Benioff Children's Hospital, San Francisco
Sally Doyle and Kathy Evans, poet-teachers

Memory

How long has it been since we stood here?
Shimmering autumn leaves drifting around us,
The sun peering through the trees in little patches of
Golden light,
Laughing at untold jokes,
Watching the hour turn to the winter sun,
The last birdcalls ringing for us.

Why did it have to end?
Seasons slipping by in a buttery haze,
Dreaming.

Has it truly left us behind?
Leaving us alone in the dark,
Trying to grasp the last of it?

How could we have forgotten?
The song of the wind,
Language of the stars,
The memory of sisterhood.

AVA NETT KRUGER
Seventh Grade, Blue Oak School, Butte County
Shannon O'Laughlin, classroom teacher
Heather Altfeld, poet-teacher

FOREIGN FEELINGS

Learning to Drive

It's like the trees by the fence
Standing bare in the middle of January
Though it's seventy-four degrees outside.
As the sun streams through
The tangled branches
Casting forlorn, sweeping shadows over the earth,
The picture doesn't add up.

It's like dreaming of flying—
One minute soaring in a practiced equilibrium
And then the next, you too, like Icarus,
Rupture this balance,
Crashing into a schoolyard fence.

It's like the time when you were six,
When your only concern was who got
To the sandbox first
Or which shovel would take you to China the fastest,
Or when you were eight
And your biggest debate was between handball and
       four-square.
Foreign feelings.

Now, as your life's trunk closes in on its sixteenth ring,
You find yourself with a palatial mass of impossibilities,

Ambiguous to the core,
As you speed down Cathedral Oaks
Learning to drive.

SOPHIA ZHENG
Tenth Grade, Music and Arts Conservatory, Santa Barbara County
Perie Longo and Chryss Yost, poet-teachers

Confusión

Yo me siento triste
when they speak Spanish
and I don't understand it.

A mí me gustaría hablar más español
Tengo tantas ganas de aprender Spanish

I can't stand it.
Cuando yo hablo en español
me confundo
and sometimes in English, too.
No quiero confundirme anymore.

I can't wait
until I learn more Spanish and English
without *confundirme*.

ABBY GOMEZ
Fifth Grade, West Marin School, Marin County
Esther Underwood, classroom teacher
Brian Kirven, poet-teacher

Rough Life

Your voice is the cement on the sidewalk
Your eyes are the bricks of a building
Your soul became the shifting rocks on a cliff
Your heart became a gravel road that I could not fall on again
Without turning black and blue
This new road could no longer catch my tears, my worries,
    or my fears
A changed man that could no more be the one I could rely on
Merely a stranger whose mind is married to the wine
Drinking the past away with a pinch of selfishness and remorse
Creating the gallons of water in rivers and lakes and seas
    and oceans
Of the family you used to have
I used to run to your embracing arms that are now filled
    with darkness
You taught me to be afraid and scared, but it made me strong
In my gallery I see pictures of you
Painful smiles
A broken violin
Shattered glass
Puzzles with the wrong pieces
Endless stairs leading down to my brokenness incomplete
They used to contain images of
Sweet cherries on a sunny day in July

Embracing the sun and capturing time with a single lens
Love and compassion in the leaves of your branches
The man you once were.

SHARON MA
Ninth Grade, Lowell High School, San Francisco
Meredith Santiago, classroom teacher
Susan Terence, poet-teacher

Adolescence

It's like this flash of red
and you fall down
shins first
a table of elbows
crying out
but you don't fall flat
you sprawl
awkwardly
you take up too much space
and sometimes you remember
to get up quick
but you're always too slow
and you always fall again
snaking, spiraling
all fingers and a thick waist
your eyes squint
you ask a lot of questions
and never get answers
you're hopeful
because your eyes are still tender
green shoots
sprouting up
leaves catching sunshine
there's so much to see
and yet
you're hardened

you've seen the view when you fall
you know your eyes are naive
you want to shove them
back into the ground
let them grow for a bit longer
but they won't listen and you cry out
when they hit the light
because
it's so much

MORGEN PACK
Twelfth Grade, Pacific Community Charter High School, Mendocino County
Yolanda Highhouse, classroom teacher
Blake More, poet-teacher

Not Mexican Enough

"But you can't be Mexican," they say,
 eyes narrowed accusingly,
 brows knit in frustration.
"But I am Mexican, if only a quarter."
 I don't look Mexican at all, with long fair hair, blue eyes,
 and whiteout skin.
 I am a patchwork quilt stitched together with the thread
 of many bloodlines.
 Each part of me is scattered throughout the world—
 a fragment in Italy, pieces in Ireland and Scotland,
 and of course, a small slice in México.

RAINI KELLOGG
Eighth Grade, West Marin School, Marin County
Julie Cassel, classroom teacher
Brian Kirven, poet-teacher

Hollow

I come from
traditional sakura trees,
glassy, cold green,
able to pull in
shadows.
Icy like the
freezing winter.
Transparent
green like the
new straws
of healthy
grass.

I was born
here for a reason.
It may still
be an undiscovered
secret, a mask
to a fear-
stricken face,
but the pain
will always
remain hidden
behind my
hollow
smiles, laughs,
words, tears.

Ice-blue Japanese
sakura flowers.
Petals dotted
with morning
dew. The color
of a tearful
raindrop. A

beautiful disaster!

LILY CHEN
Fifth Grade, Francis Scott Key Elementary, San Francisco
Michelle Lee, classroom teacher
Susan Terence, poet-teacher

Divorce

Divorce is a painful thing to deal with.
When bad things happen between your parents,

it affects your life, their lives, your family's life.
It feels like a heavy stone, weighing you down

on the cold floor, breaking you
into pieces. Every feeling so strong

and powerful. Sometimes your parents take turns
and sometimes you're separated from one parent
and always with the other.

Divorce brings sadness, but one day
you must let the pain flow behind you.

I know it's hard, but you must let go
to go on with your life.

LEA ROBBINS
Fifth Grade, Cold Spring School, Santa Barbara County
Joel Orr, classroom teacher
Perie Longo, poet-teacher

if it makes you less sad

you've been in
this pit of depression
for weeks   you're

down, i know but
we care about you.
we don't want to
see you like this.
i kid you   not

dear, i know
this is hard & you're
tempted
he left so you're
leaving yourself scars
but i can relate
i also feel quite   alone

i'm banging on your
door,
i hear nothing.
you won't let me   in

you're lying on the
ground. but you aren't
breathing,
you woke up the
next day,
but don't take life
so seriously, be strong
you can pull through   this

CASSIE SPENCER
Ninth Grade, Eel River Community School, Humboldt County
Felicia Doherty, classroom teacher
Dan Zev Levinson, poet-teacher

I Am a Fool

Life is like a swimming pool.
When it is full, life is cool.
When it's dry,
I get out my skateboard
and fill the pool with curves, carves,
and my own blood
because I am a fool.

DAVID
West Hills High School, Mendocino County
Rich Bowen, classroom teacher
Bill Jabez Churchill, poet-teacher

Red Eyes

Red eyes
Crying out blood
Coughing hard, no true love
Trying to get away from drugs
These streets

RAY RHODES
Tenth Grade, Mendocino Sunrise High School, Mendocino County
Elise Boyle and Doug Nunn, classroom teachers
Emily Inwood, poet-teacher

Black

Oh, black,
You are the one who I feared most as a child
You made me tremble at night
Over time I have grown to love you and use you to my
    advantage
Through moonlight you creep and crawl through the
    trees and curtains
Like a wave of black hawks you raid through the night
and cut through the light like a stainless-steel knife
How I wish I could be with you and be as dark and cold
    as you
Without you I would be covered in light,
without you I would be weak.
I awake to your anxiety.

TONI DORIN
Eleventh Grade, San Rafael High School, Marin County
Evan Boris, classroom teacher
Claire Blotter, poet-teacher

No One Knows

No one knows
who I really am.
Everyone sees me
as a shy girl
who never cries,
who never gets angry.
When my
feelings are hurt,
I keep my tears inside
and when something
makes me angry,
flames burn inside,
all full of
words of hatred.
I am a locked-up box.
Where's the key?
I don't know.
I don't think it was ever made.
Never, ever.

MONICA MARTELL
Fourth Grade, Marquez Charter, Los Angeles County
Lynne Wilkinson, classroom teacher
Michelle Bitting, poet-teacher

Her Eyes
based on a family photo

This is my father.
His hair is still full
and black.
His eyes worn
from the tiring nights.
His smile is so big
because he is now a father.
Chest hair crawls out
from his white henley shirt.
His skin is
a rusty brown tone.

This is me.
I am a baby.
My tiny hands
are trying to grip his huge hand.
My lips are pink,
like roses.
My eyes are dark brown,
having the same tired, dazed look.
My skin is
pale.

As years pass,
his smile wears away into
a scorn.

A scorn that scorns
fingerpaint on walls.
A scorn that scorns
the stealing of two more cookies.
I get more rebellious as I grow.

MARIJKE PIETERS-KWIERS
Sixth Grade, Sinaoloa Middle, Marin County
Tracy Walker, classroom teacher
Lea Aschkenas, poet-teacher

Silence

Silence is a dark room
filled with nothing
except a pitch-black
monster called
the imprisoned.
And there is
a consequence.
The imprisoned
is
my father.
My father is
like a black violet
locked in a closet
who has never
seen daylight.
Wherever he is,
it is forever
silent.

NYAH LUND LOVERGINE
Fifth Grade, Dana Gray Elementary, Mendocino County
Barbara Stone, classroom teacher
Karen Lewis, poet teacher

The Caterpillar

The little critter drags across
a leaf, munching
every
bit of it.
The
caterpillar
hides in
his cozy
chrysalis, patiently
waiting
for its evolution.
In about a week the moment
has come, he spreads
out his crisp wings
ready to go
and bathes them
in the golden sunlight. The caterpillar who is
now not a caterpillar takes flight with tender
wings ready to go. He drifts off to the sky, leaving
shiny sprinkles behind him. I
wish I wasn't a late bloomer.

CHRISTOPHER M. FONG
Fifth Grade, Hoover Elementary School, Santa Clara County
Mrs. Sheldon, classroom teacher
Gail Newman, poet-teacher

The Wind Is at My Back
a mirror sonnet

The wind is at my back
as I turn to walk away.
You probably feel deserted.
Well, I feel betrayed.
You made me a promise
and then you walked away.
I thought I was important.

I thought I was important
and then you walked away.
You made me a promise.
Well, I feel betrayed.
You probably feel deserted
as I turn to walk away.
The wind is at my back.

INDIA ALLEN
Seventh Grade, Coastal Grove Charter School, Humboldt County
Shana Langer, classroom teacher
Julie Hochfeld, poet-teacher

The Starry Night
after Vincent van Gogh's 1889 painting

A fire had erupted
The night sky had a heavy wind
The moon blazed like the sun
People in the town were all awake
Wondering what to do
Lights all on
Children huddled next to their parents
It was terrifying,
But at the same time, beautiful
The stars, very bright, shone on the rolling hills
Then came a shooting star, and everything silenced
And the sky became dark except for
The stars that burned brightly all night

SKYLA BERTSCH
Seventh Grade, Coastal Grove Charter School, Humboldt County
Jenny Rushby, classroom teacher
Julie Hochfeld, poet-teacher

THE WIND THAT TRAVELS THE WORLD

The Wind of the World

I am the wind that travels the world.
I go into buildings, then out again.
Can anyone be better than me?
I think everyone wants to be me.
I'd blow it to them.
If they don't know where to go
I'd show it to them.

PARMVIR SINGH
Fifth Grade, Buri Buri Elementary School, South San Francisco
Lynn Rivera, classroom teacher
Maureen Hurley, poet-teacher

Slanted

i am fresh off a plane, wings longing to fly back to muddy
tangled roads and familiar *long gnan* branches
twisted beautifully
captivated by the southward smiling sun
i am the atmosphere of a sweatshop
last to the cloth bin doesn't get to pay rent
i am love letters from my mother to my father
traveling halfway around the world
stuck between business proposals and
envelopes filled with greasy money
finding their way to greedy fingertips
traveling halfway around the world to find open hands and
hungry mouths
lips
i am spring grass, pushing its way up from the unrelenting
dark soil
being talked to by the gentle words of my once-young
       grandfather
practicing his speech
hand movements unlike his father
i've known clicking locks and half-wide-open doors
i've spent countless hours painting orange magnolias on
       paper umbrellas
to understand me you must gather all your
blankets and mattresses
go into the alley, do not look back
they're here

i am the daughter of fear
fear of
what if the Japanese find me
what if God isn't real
what if i never bear a son
what if my feet still don't fit those shoes
i am the daughter of church bells echoing through the
      humid air
of firecrackers and sweet frozen green bean popsicles
i am the daughter of slanted eyes, but they don't
      undermine my vision

ANITA CHEN
Ninth Grade, Lowell High School, San Francisco
Timothy Lamarre, classroom teacher
Susan Terence, poet-teacher

The Moment When You Look Up at the Clouds and Say "I Am"

I am a glance, a pause, a question,
a faded Star of David,
an uprooted live-oak tree.

I am bare feet on grass, cinnamon bun Kentucky where
fireflies flit and light the evening with
false shimmer.
I am San Francisco of Castro fairs, graffiti art,
      and familiar floating fog.

I'm the lost breath as the sun rises
(sky flushed pink-red and golden beams blazing, splitting
and conquering the night as they mellow into a
      watercolor blue).

I am a sad smile at the stars.

I am a single heartbeat, lost and found in the noise,
a drop in the ocean of
the city of hate and love,
simply a fleeting human (there one day, gone the next).

I am a cozy gray hoodie, a worn pink blanket.
I am one step closer to a distant rainbow.

I am a tired sigh,
a hopeful glance.

I am wondering tears, after all,
the universe is so very big, and I
am so very small.

ZOE KAISER
Ninth Grade, Lowell High School, San Francisco
Meredith Santiago, classroom teacher
Susan Terence, poet-teacher

Joyful Dolphin

I am the dolphin of joy.
I learned to rule the waves
from the crescent moon.
I taught the rain to fall
as smooth as skin.
I am the patience of the ocean.

Masaya na Lumba-Lumba

Ako ay isang lumba-lumba ng kasiyahan.
Natutunan kong pamunuan ang
Mula sa paglaki ng bunan.
Tinuran ko ang ulan na bumagsak
Katulag ng balat na makinis.
Ako ang pasensya ng karagatan.

JENNA STA. MARIA
Fifth Grade, Buri Buri Elementary School, South San Francisco
Lynn Rivera, classroom teacher
Maureen Hurley, poet-teacher
Tagalog translation by Nessie Sta. Maria

The Great Bird

A bird, all life on the tips of its wings.
If it flaps its wings, a giant earthquake
cracks the earth in two.
Where is this great bird?
I will search in the sky and deep into the earth.
I pray this bird will soon be upon me.
I am old and gray from looking,
but I will search for this wonderful bird
until the end of time.
I am still full of hope.

QUINN HORAK
Second Grade, Oak Grove School, Sonoma County
Ellen Douglass, classroom teacher
Phyllis Meshulam, poet-teacher

Ancestors

I hear the ancestors
In the red rocks and boulders.
Over the clouds and under the moon.
Hiding in the fire
and under the ground.

Ancestors are still there
but cannot be seen.
They hide in the dark
shadows. In the woods and
in the shallow water of
life. All over the place,
even in the flower buds.

ALI ALI
Fourth Grade, Lakeshore Elementary School, San Francisco
Sheila Tenney, classroom teacher
Grace Grafton, poet-teacher

In Our Dreams

From 1910–1940, over 50,000 Chinese immigrants entering the United States were held at Angel Island. Most often, men made the journey alone and remained separated from their families for many years.

I. Child's View

In my dreams
I see my father
coming home
from America
rich with gold.
I will run into his arms
laughing with joy.
He will tell me
of blue waves
and strange Americans.
His laughs are
like thunder.
His cooking like
heaven.
I miss his
tanned skin,
black hair,
brown eyes.
But it is all a
dream.

II. Father's View

In my dreams
I see my family.
My wife laughing
at me.
My sister
cooking dinner.
But most of all,
my daughter
curling on my lap
listening to my stories
with those bright
shining eyes.
After I'm finished,
she'll beg me
for another.
In these dreams,
I forget my suffering,
where I am,
and most of all,
separation from my family.

TIFFANY TANG
Fifth Grade, Francis Scott Key Elementary, San Francisco
Michelle Lee, classroom teacher
Susan Terence, poet-teacher

Bearded Man with a Cardboard Box

The man we always walk past,
who is playing the saxophone
or the drums,

the person with the cardboard box
and the basket filled with Top Ramen,
broken beach toys, glass bottles.
Their signs say:
Just Lost Job
or
Five Kids.

Sometimes I wonder
if they will make it
or how they even got there.

Adults say
"They did stupid things.
Don't ever be like them."
But really...
weren't they once
like me?

GRANT SHAIN
Seventh Grade, Rancho Santa Fe Middle School, San Diego County
Alison Murphy, classroom teacher
Jackleen Holton, poet-teacher

Red White Blue

They view cultures nowadays
As angered and crazed
Society has lapses
America's lost passion
Industries rise
While citizens are crashing
It will be our demise
But we're blind to the government's masking
What defines an assassin—
Someone who kills someone with political power and the society they devour?
My words will surely leave Congress's faces soured,
But I'm standing up for myself,
I will not stand behind
You cowards.

DANIN TYRRELL
Eleventh Grade, Willits High School, Mendocino County
Jeff Bergman, classroom teacher
PJ Flowers, poet-teacher

The Sound

I am the sound
that makes your chest shake
the pounding of feet on the floor
teaches me to keep beating
small moving lights twirl around the room
encouraging people to move
sitting in the back
I educate knees to bounce
I am the vibration, the vibration
in the concrete when a car goes by
rattling your bones
and etching a sketch in your mind
I am the sound of a rainbow
utter silence
teaching us to dream
while we're awake
I am the sound
that makes your chest shake

CELESTE VAN ABRAMS
Tenth Grade, Pacific Community Charter High School, Mendocino County
Yolanda Highhouse, classroom teacher
Blake More, poet-teacher

Until I Saw

Until I saw a snowflake
I never knew the sub-zero
beauty of a tiny crystal of ice

Until I saw the desert
I never knew that wind could
erode rocks and turn them
into a sea of sand that held
the most amazing creatures

Until I saw lightning
I never knew the loud power
of the sky as it flashed
its rage at the earth below

CASMALI LOPEZ
Fourth Grade, Montecito Union School, Santa Barbara County
Heidi Craine, classroom teacher
Lois Klein, poet-teacher

Sun of Happiness

The sun of happiness brings light and joy
to the sorrowful and the lost.

May the rays of light guide a man
through the thickest forest of his darkest hour,
and let hope and joy be bestowed upon
the weak and hopeless.

In hopes the sun of happiness may
create a land of peace
and violence be cast away
into the lake of forgotten tragedy.

MICHAEL TRUONG
Sixth Grade, Pomeroy Elementary, Santa Clara County
Sandra Armstrong, classroom teacher
Mara Sheade, poet-teacher

The Island of a Vegetable

A road leads to nowhere
        Circling 'round and 'round
An eye watches you
        Brown continents in a white ocean
An old, overused hat sits on its head
        Bruised, scarred
Wise and ancient
        A small island in a sea of brown, dirty water
Only two houses create the population
        One is rundown and poor
The other a magnificent mansion
        Nobody bothers to clean the road
Smooth, sandy and rough
        All together, a mixed feeling
Cold, soft, yet hard
        Its earthy perfume envelops it
        Patiently waiting
        Future unknown

RACHEL CHIANG
Sixth Grade, Pomeroy Elementary, Santa Clara County
Sandra Armstrong, classroom teacher
Mara Sheade, poet-teacher

Polar Bear

I see white trees all around me.
I hear shuffling snow.
I smell pine trees as green as fresh grass.
I feel soft, clean snow beneath me.
I taste raw seal meat.
I imagine it being a better life.
It doesn't seem too nice up here in the Arctic ice.
I want to be somewhere where it is not five degrees below zero.
My cub is snuggled up tight to me.
Apparently, he doesn't like it here either.

MATTHEW CANDAU
Third Grade, Gravenstein Elementary, Sonoma County
Kasey Hillier, classroom teacher
Iris Jamahl Dunkle, poet-teacher

How to Be the Moon

Keep pulling and pushing the azure waves.

Remember to shine silver in the night
        while other beings fall into a deep, dreamy sleep.

Allow yourself to only sometimes
        let your full glow illuminate the ebony midnight.

Look for all spidery and sinister doings
        with your subtle light.

Wonder about and peer into those little humans' big dreams.
        What imagination they have!

Feel the slow turning of the planet
        you take a turn watching over.

Hear only the noise the snowy owl makes,
        a low hoot.

Be the moon, be yourself!

NATASHA WEISS
Fourth Grade, Crane Country Day School, Santa Barbara County
Stephanie Bagish, classroom teacher
Lois Klein, poet-teacher

Lighthouse Hill
inspired by an Edward Hopper painting

Curved mountains
blue sky
clean grass
mountains curve like waves
blue sky standing on top of the world
together

The lighthouse is high and big
Every day we see a beautiful blue sky
No one is with us
Every day you look like the sun
rising up high in the sky

We had a family that lived here with us
Then they vanished into thin air
Now we wait here forever

About twenty years later
the boy from the family is now a gentleman
He swears to live with us forever

Sixty years have passed, the gentleman
turned into an old man
One day he went for a walk
When he came back, he wrote a letter
but I couldn't read it because it was too dark

I didn't see him walk out of the door in the morning
I still wait for him until that day
A storm comes
the lightning hits me
I'm burned by lightning
Slowly, I have gone forever
No one, no one knows what he wrote

NHAT NGUYEN
Sixth Grade, John Muir Middle School, Alameda County
Jen Achten, classroom teacher
Kristin Palm, poet-teacher

The Sun

The sun is on the move
jumping and skipping across the sky.
He hears music,
the music of the wind,
blowing about like cool jazz,
the music of the birds,
first soft, like a crooning,
then loud, bubbling out its throat,
the music of the sun itself, glowing out of a mouth
of nonexistence, filling the day
with light, making people around the world laugh.

OCEANA ORTIZ
Fifth Grade, Springhill School, Contra Costa County
Deborah Hungerford, classroom teacher
J. Ruth Gendler, poet-teacher

Chasm

I watched as a feather fell from the hawk,
Like a stone echoes down an endless chasm,
Drifting down like clouds across the sky.
Falling in endless harmony, yet in infinite discord.
I am but a speck of nothing,
I've strayed from my safe haven, now I'm alone.

I have been given the bones of the earth,
I have the sinews of the universe at my disposal.
Like the dew on the morning grass,
Some things cannot exist without each other
Like death cannot exist without life.
Without blood in our veins the universe is blind.

In a land of endless ice, where sky is mere shadow.
Spirits dance in shades of purple, red & blue.
In the darkness, stars are beacons of light.
Within the clouds lies an ocean.
Under the ground lies a river of ash like a snake.
All around are mountains of rock, plains.
Above it is the open sky.

AMANDA HAVER
Fifth Grade, Buri Buri Elementary School, South San Francisco
Chris Stone, classroom teacher
Maureen Hurley, poet-teacher

Raining Baseballs
inspired by a postcard

In the sky there is a baseball-shaped cloud.
It is raining baseballs everywhere.
Kids race outside to catch them
as they fall from the sky.

I see the chaos of people running
and throwing the balls. I smell the fragrance
of fresh grass that covers the baseballs
as they fall fast to the hard, wet ground.

I taste the delicious eggs Mom has made
as I watch the street through our kitchen window.
In my imagination I taste popcorn, crackerjacks,
hot dogs, cotton candy, and roasted peanuts.

LEON WU
Fourth Grade, Spreckels Elementary School, San Diego County
Elizabeth Stewart, classroom teacher
Seretta Martin, poet-teacher

Flyball

I wish I were a gold ball
Soaring over third base
   in the afternoon.

I wish I were a silver bat
hitting a ball flying higher
  than the Big Dipper
  floating in black space.

I wish I were the orange planets
  watching the ball
  fly over the white clouds.

CASSADY KOMATER
Second Grade, New Traditions Elementary, San Francisco
Gina Robertson, classroom teacher
Susan Terence, poet-teacher

Out of This World

Space is aglow with planets and stars.
Some, one million times bigger than Earth
or as small as a dime.
If I could visit space,
I would spot the constellations,
Cancer, Capricorn, and Orion the Hunter.
When I see the stars,
I wonder if aliens are actually out there.
Not bad, not good, somewhere in between.

In a spaceship flying like a speeding bullet,
maybe even faster,
I would travel through giant galaxies like a snake
slithering in and out of a hole.
I would go farther than anyone has ever gone.

I would take photographs
that would become world famous
and last forever.
I would dig through the moon
and find what no one has found before.
There would be a mystery in space
and I would solve it.

Space is an amazing place to go.

FINN BAKER
Third Grade, Coleman School, Marin County
Renee Stender, classroom teacher
Michele Rivers, poet-teacher

I Am the World

I am a huge, strong planet. I wonder
if I am the largest thing around.

I hear men and women talking about planets.
I see nothing but a glow from far away.

I want to see down inside of myself.
I am the world.

I feel sad that I can't know
what it is like to be a person.

I say to you, "I will never die,
but this rotation is boring me."

I dream of doing something exciting.
Someday I hope to become famous.

Be kind to me. I am the world.

TRENT JOHNSON
Third Grade, Spreckels Elementary School, San Diego County
Marisela Sparks, classroom teacher
Seretta Martin, poet-teacher

California Poets in the Schools
Poet-Teachers 2011–12

ALAMEDA COUNTY
J. Ruth Gendler, Grace Grafton, Maureen Hurley,
Tobey Kaplan, Alison Luterman, Tureeda Mikell,
Kristin Palm, Mara Sheade, Marissa Bell Toffoli

BUTTE & TEHAMA COUNTIES
Heather Altfeld

CONTRA COSTA COUNTY
J. Ruth Gendler, Maureen Hurley, Alison Seevak

HUMBOLDT COUNTY
Daryl Ngee Chinn, Julie Hochfeld, Daniel Zev Levinson

INYO COUNTY
Eva Poole-Gilson

LAKE COUNTY
Michele Krueger

LOS ANGELES COUNTY
Michelle Bitting, Fernando Castro, Nels Christianson,
David Del Bourgo, Tresha Haefner, Alice Pero, India Radfar

MADERA COUNTY
L. Anne Molin

MARIN COUNTY
Lea Aschkenas, Karen Benke, Duane Big Eagle,
Claire Blotter, Sasha Eakle, Kathy Evans, Terri Glass,
Brian Kervin, Michele Rivers, Prartho Sereno,
giovanni singleton

MENDOCINO COUNTY
Jabez W. Churchill, PJ Flowers, Emily Inwood, Karen Lewis,
Blake More, Chris Olander, Dan Roberts

NEVADA, PLACER & SIERRA COUNTIES
Chris Olander, Will Staple, Julie Valin

SACRAMENTO COUNTY
JoAnn Anglin

SAN BENITO COUNTY
Amanda Chiado

SAN DIEGO COUNTY
Christina Burress, Brandon Cesmat, Veronica Cunningham, Shadab Zeest Hashmi, minerva (Gail) Hawkins, Jackleen Holton, Seretta Martin, Jill Moses, Johnnierenee Nelson, Claudia Poquoc, Celia Sigmon

SAN FRANCISCO COUNTY
Laura Davis, Sally Doyle, Claudia Dudley, Kathy Evans, Grace Grafton, Dawn Marie Knopf, Karen Llagas, devorah major, D. Scot Miller, Gail Newman, Susan Sibbet, Susan Terence, J.T. Teodoro

SAN MATEO COUNTY
Emmanuel Williams

SANTA BARBARA COUNTY
Christine Kravetz, Lois Klein, Perie Longo, Melinda Palacio, Chryss Yost

SANTA CLARA COUNTY
Gail Newman

SHASTA & SISKIYOU COUNTIES
Beth Beurkens, Dan Zev Levinson

SONOMA COUNTY
Molly Albracht-Sierra, Arthur Dawson, Claire Drucker, Iris Jamahl Dunkle, Meg Hamill, Maureen Hurley, Phyllis Meshulam, Gwynn O'Gara, Christina Perez, Pamela Singer Yezbick

VENTURA COUNTY
Tree Bernstein, Richard Newsham, Shelley Savren

YOLO COUNTY
Eve West Bessier

California Poets in the Schools

BOARD OF DIRECTORS, 2011–12
Christina Chang, Daryl Ngee Chinn, Nels Christianson,
Anna diMartino, Jamie Jordan, Michele Krueger,
Karen Lewis, Jill Moses, Prithvi Nobuth, Susan Sibbet

HAAS BOARD FELLOWS, 2011–12
Gaurav Agarwal, Peter Rhee

ADVISORY COUNCIL
Cathy Barber, Carol Muske Dukes, Kathy Evans,
Katharine Harer, Jane Hirshfield, Patricia Holland,
Christine Kravetz, Kayla Krut, Philip Levine, devorah major,
Sara McAulay, David Sibbet, Anne Smith, Al Young

STAFF
Tina Areja-Pasquinzo, Joy Estudillo

VOLUNTEERS
Amanda Chun, Stephanie Ma, Jack Murphy, Holly Orr,
Kennedy Pasquinzo, Nicholas Pasquinzo, Cindy Wong,
Milton Wong, Carrie Yu

Acknowledgments

The California Arts Council supports classroom workshops, statewide training and networking, and hosts Poetry Out Loud to live audiences in high schools and beyond. *Turning Into Stars* came to print because generous benefactors value the creative talents and intellectual curiosity of young writers. Thank you.

ANGELS
Anonymous (3), Cathy Barber & Alan Brenner, Daryl & Phyllis Chinn, Gordon Davies, Ken Haas, Susan & David Sibbet

MUSES
Valerie Berry, Carolyn Bollinger, Donald & Ruby Branson, Lee Doan, Kathy Evans, Barbara Ann Frank, Marvin Hoffenberg, Daniel Meisel & Amy Wendel, Stephanie Mendel, Ruth Sherer, Peter B. Wiley

STARS
Sharon Beckman, Elizabeth & Park Chamberlain, Christina Chang, Nancy & Dale Dougherty, Gail Entrekin, Mr. & Mrs. A. Lee Follett, Saori Fujitani, Shelby & Frederick Gans, Alison Geballe, Anne Harper, Barbara A. Hughes, Raymond Lifchez, Nina Lindsay, Nion McEvoy

LAUREATES
Gaurav Agarwal, Thomas Bénét, Laura & Scott Cooper, Eleanor & Francis Ford Coppola, Milton Chen & Ruth Cox, Nels Christianson, Dorothy Dumas, Iris Dunkle, Annette Bianchi & Sara Furrer, Mary Lee Gowland, Daria Joseph, Christine Kravetz, Kelly Ilnicki & Mark Lambert, Chris Marshall, Prithvi Nobuth, Michele Rivers, Jean Schulz, Shelly Sharp, Jan Woodward Stevenson, Roselyne C. Swig, Sylvia Wong & March Helfman

PATRONS
Beulah Amsterdam, Emily Anicich, Yoel Kahn & Dan Bellm, A.S. & Jeanne Bennion, Lewis Sargentich & Valerie Bradley, Jennifer Swanton Brown, Lola Brown, Colleen Busch, Carol Ann Casner, Thomas Caudle, Tina Cervin, Antoinette Constaple, Robert Cox, Katherine & Gregg Crawford, Arthur Dawson, Carole Deitrich, Sally Doyle, Marta Drury, Eleanor Dwight, Richard Dysart & Kathryn Jacobi Dysart, Victoria Ehrlich, Jane Elsdon, Sandra K. Erickson, Lisa A. Ezzard, David & Vicki Fleishhacker, Sandra Florstedt & Bill Davidson, Rebecca Foust, Ellen Geohegan, J. Ruth Gendler, Bernard Gershenson & Paula Gocker, Michael Gioia, Dale & Philip Going, Ethel Goldsmith, Ronda Gomez-Quinones, Roselee Greenholtz, Karen Harber, Jane & Kevin Hart, Brenda Hillman & Robert Hass, Lyn Hejinian, Jane Hirshfield,

Sandra Hoben, Chris Holland, Jackleen Holton, Torre C. Houlgate-West, Maureen Hurley, Carol Kent Ireland & Uncle Don B. Fanning, Rebecca Jennings & Walter Mann, Valerie Johns, Debra Johnson, MD, George & Sylvia Johnson, Louise Jordan, Barbara & Jim Jourdonnais, Linda Judd, Jane Kaplan & Donatello Bonato, Dorothy Kravetz, Eric & Katharine Kravetz, Joan Kreiss, Jacqueline Kudler, C. Y. Leong, Lynn & David Loux, Helen S. & Leon J. Luey, Robert McLaughlin, Phyllis Meshulam, Michael Miller, L. Anne Molin, Diane Moore, Henry Morro, Jill Moses, Gail Newman, Nancy W. Newmeyer, Mike & Judy O'Shea, Chris Olander, Felicia Oldfather, Michael Allen Orend, Ruth Palmer, William Pattengill, Sheila & Stephen Petrarca, Frances Phillips, Ira & Edith Plotinsky, John Porter, Neal Powers, Kim Probst, Elizabeth Quintella, Lynne Rappaport, Eleanor Reich, Barbara & Nigel Renton, Ivy & Leigh Robinson, Lawrence Robinson, Susan & Andre Roegiers, Eva Schlesinger, Susie Schlesinger, Ruth & Alan Scott, Alison Seevak, Gerrett Snedaker & Diane Krause, Susan Spencer, Susan E. Stewart, Gretchen Stone, Patrice Warrender, Katherine Willens, Michael Witlin, Laurel Witrow, Steven Wright, Tanya Zimmer, Patti & John Zussman

FRIENDS
Molly Albracht Sierra, Laura Alonso, Heather Altfeld, Leonard Anderson, Richard & M. Natica Angilly, JoAnn M. Anglin, Carol Anton, Linda Artel & Bruce Berg, Lea Aschkenas, Mary K. Baird, Loan Baranow, Richard Beard, Judy Bebelaar, Karen Benke, Marlene Benke, Sara Benson, Tree Bernstein, Eve West Bessier, Beth Beurkens, Duane BigEagle, Bernice Biggs, Michelle Bitting, Claire Blotter, Lorraine Bonner, Lynne & Michael Braverman, Joyce Bryson, Christina Burress, Timothy Cabrera, Robert Carroll, MD, Uldine Castel, Fernando Castro, Phyllis Cath, Brandon Cesmat, Amanda Chiado, Clarissa Chin, Jabez (Bill) Churchill, Jacqueline Colburn, Christopher Michael Collins, Beverly Coughlin, Susan & David Courrejou, Beth-Marie Deenihan, Janet DeBar, Albert Flynn DeSilver, David Del Bourgo, Carolyn Dickinson, Patricia & Ted Dienstfrey, Ed & Verity Dierauf, Ellen Dillinger, Claire Drucker, Claudia Dudley, Richard Dysart & Kathryn Jacobi Dysart, Sasha Eakle, Catherine Edgett, Jeffrey Embleton, James & Dorothy Fadiman, Melissa Fafarman, Wendy Fisher, Jacquelyn Fiske Laso, Janet Fitch, Stewart Florsheim, Phyllis Flowers, Leah J. Forbes, Donna Franzblau, William Gainer, Joan Gelfand, Terri Glass, Mary Lee Gowland, Grace Grafton, Roselee Greenholtz, Susan & Gary Gulbransen, Clair Gustafson, William & Patricia Hager, Megan Hamill, Shadab Zeest Hashmi, Minerva Hawkins, Anne A. Helms, Suki Hill, Judith & Michael Hill-Weld, Julie Hochfeld, Patricia Holland, Barbara Holman, Terry Horrigan, Glenna B. Horton, Elijah Imlay, Georgette James, Alice & Dale Johnson, John Johnson & Sarah Hensel, Suzanne Titus Johnson, Troy Jollimore, Georgia Jones, Dorothea Joos, Gail Kabat,

Tobey Kaplan, Joan H. Kip, Brian Kirven, Lois Klein, Dawn Marie Knopf, Robert Kosturak, Richard Krejsa, MD, Marilyn Kriegel, Michele Krueger, Kayla & Mary Ellen Krut, Maxine Landis, Christine Landon, Dorothy Langlois, Lanny Larson & Lynne Rodriguez, Andrew Leavitt, MD, Emily W. Leider, Lucia Lemieux, Lisa Lethin, Daniel Zev Levinson, Sylvia H. Levinson, Rosanne & Alvin Levitt, Karen Lewis, Wendy Lichtman, Peter Linenthal, Michele Linfante, Karen Llagas, Christina Lloyd, Dana Lomax, Perie Longo, Bruce Lyall, Yvonne Lyerla, Teresa McNeil MacLean, Susan Maeder, devorah major, Jerry Martien, Robyn Martin, Seretta Martin, Yvonne Mason, Michael McLaughlin, Mary Lee McNeal, Teresa McNeil MacLean, Alexa Mergen, Eliška Meyers, Tureeda Mikell, Joe Milosch, Marian & Philip Miller, Magdalena Montagne, Blake More, Rene Moreno Silva, Deborah Morris, Elli Nagai-Rothe, Tomi Nagai-Rothe, Brenda Nasio, Johnnierenee Nelson, Richard Newsham, Liz Nichols, Gwynn O'Gara, Kirsten Ogden, Marc Olmsted, Christine Orr, Melinda Palacio, Pauline Pao, Margot Pepper, Christina Perez, Alice Pero, Daniel Polikof, Claudia Poquoc, Yvonne Postelle, Sharon Pretti, India T. Radfar, Carlos Ramirez, Janet Rice, Gabrielle Rilleau, Michele Rivers, Kim Rosen, Sarah Rosenthal, Robert & Susan Roth, Greg Barsh & Carolyn Russo, Joyce Sabel, Bruce J. Sams, Roussel Sargent, Shelley Savren, Dennis & Loretta Schmitz, Prartho Sereno, Mara Sheade, Eliza Shefler, Celia Sigmon, Murray & Marsha Silverstein, John Oliver Simon, giovanni singleton, Elijah Smith, Lise-Lotte Smith, Regina Sneed, Gary Snyder, Julia Springer, Bob Stanley, Will Staple, Mary Stein, Hannah Stein, David Charles Taylor, David Tejeda & Jude Deckenbach, Susan Terence, Marcia Thompson, Marissa Bell Toffoli, Centa Theresa Uhalde, Julie Valin, Eloise Van Tassel, Florence Weinberger, Al Weinrub, Karen Cross Whyte, Emmanuel Williams, Susan Wooldridge, Mitsuye May Yamada, Steven Louie & Karen Yee, Pamela Singer Yezbick, Chryss Yost, Angela Yuan, Susan Zegans

GOVERNMENT, FOUNDATION & BUSINESS SUPPORTERS
Anonymous, Arena Theater Association, Art House Los Angeles, Association of Writers & Writing Programs, Barnes and Noble, Beyond Baroque, The Blackie Foundation, Books Inc., The Branson Foundation, California Arts Council, Center for Cultural Innovation, Cheshire Bookshop, City of San Buenaventura, City of San Rafael, City Lights Bookstore, Communication Catalysts, Inc., Community Foundation Sonoma County, Community Thrift Store, The Companion Group, Dougherty Family Fund, The Richard F. Dwyer - Eleanor W. Dwyer Fund, Entrekin Family Foundation, Escape From New York Pizza, eScrip, Fine Arts Museums of San Francisco, FLOCKworks, The Frank Foundation, Frankie's Pizza, French Garden Restaurant, Gallery Bookshop, The Grove Consultants International, Walter & Elise Haas Fund, Harvest Market, James Irvine Foundation, KidQuake,

LitQuake, Marin Community Foundation, Dave & Roma McCoy Family Foundation, Mendocino County Office of Education, Mill Valley Market, Inc., Muller Family Foundation, National Endowment for the Arts, Pacific Palisades Library, PEN Center USA, Poetry Flash, Poets & Writers, Robinson Family Trust, Rotary Club of Mendocino, Rotary Club of Sebastopol, San Diego Border Voices, San Francisco Giants Community Fund, San Francisco Public Library, San Francisco Unified School District, Santa Barbara Museum of Art, Sher-Right Fund, Dan D. Smith & Joan Marler-Smith Fund, Sidney Stern Memorial Trust, UCSF Benioff Children's Hospital, Ventura Community Foundation, Watershed Festival, Woodward Family Foundation, Zellerbach Family Foundation, the Arts Councils of Alameda, Humboldt, Lake, Madera, Marin, Mendocino, Sacramento, San Diego, Santa Barbara, San Luis Obispo, and Sonoma Counties

Our Mission

Founded in 1964, California Poets in the Schools is one of the largest literary artists-in-residence programs in the nation. We encourage students throughout California to recognize and celebrate their creativity, intuition, and intellectual curiosity through the creative writing process. CPITS serves students in hundreds of public and private schools, juvenile halls, after-school programs, hospitals, and other community settings. We also work with the California Arts Council to bring the Poetry Out Loud recitation program to high schools and audiences throughout the state.

Our visiting poet-teachers are professional, published writers who are trained in the art of teaching poetry at age-appropriate levels. They affirm the cultural diversity of California by sharing its multicultural literary heritage with students. Our goal is to make curriculum-enriching poetry workshops available to every student in California.

To order copies of *Turning into Stars* and to discover other resources for young writers, please contact us:

California Poets in the Schools
1333 Balboa Street, #3
San Francisco, CA 94118
(415) 221-4201
www.cpits.org

Coming Soon to a High School Near You!

Poetry Out Loud, presented in partnership with the California Arts Council, the National Endowment for the Arts, and the Poetry Foundation, is a national program that encourages high school students to learn about great poetry through memorization, performance, and competition.

Poetry Out Loud is a natural complement to creative writing workshops.

To sign up your school please contact California Poets in the Schools or the California Arts Council. We are partnering to bring this extraordinary opportunity to all California high schools statewide.

info@cpits.org (Tina Pasquinzo)
kmargolis@cac.ca.gov (Kristin Margolis)
www.cac.ca.gov/poetryoutloud